THE OTHER SIDE OF *Midnight*

Extraordinary Praise for

THE OTHER SIDE OF MIDNIGHT:
A 21-Day Fasting Guide to Life Transformation

Dr. Angel White's *21-Day Fasting Guide* has stretched me beyond my normal capacity. Since I have been engaging in her declarations and inspirational teachings, my relationship with God has acquired depth and elevation concerning His purposes for my life. I'm grateful for the challenge to learn about our savior, Jesus Christ through Hebraic roots that started as a fast but transcends to a lifestyle. Thank you, Dr. Angel White for the stretch in 2019.

—Tanya Jefferson

Dr. Angel White, your obedience to God is remarkable. Your willingness to commit to this 21-day journey and be the conduit by which God used to invite others is admirable. It has truly been a blessing to be a benefactor of such a great teaching. My life has been enriched even the more because of this 21-day journey! In your voice, "Here we go." Thank you!

—Min Patricia Wade

The 21-day fast has help me come to the realization that I needed these devotionals. I've been reminded that I shouldn't call myself anything less than what my Father calls me. You will find rich treasure as you search your own heart and it will be well worth it.

—Pastor Kim White

Dr. White is definitely one of the most inspirational people I have ever known. Her 21-day fast and the messages that are attached has really strengthened me to do some of the things that I know God has called me to do. The messages have given clarity and direction to intentionally meditate on certain areas. The messages that are attached were always in line with what God was speaking to me personally. It is wonderful that she made this public on social media because it impacts so many. May God bless Dr. White, and I pray that all she is seeking after God for He will continue to reveal His perfect will for her life.

—Minister Arifah Goodwin

Fasting is such a powerful tool that enables one to strengthen their intimacy with God while simultaneously providing holistic development to oneself. This opportunity of sacrifice is a sure way for anyone to receive clarity and direction from God about their life. Fasting is extremely challenging, but these challenges can be subdued with a fasting devotional. On many occasions, I've used fasting devotionals as a guide for my consecration. These particular devotionals assisted me with daily scriptures and positive thoughts for meditation. Whenever I felt tempted to deviate from my fast, I would recall those words of empowerment to sustain me. I recommend a devotional for fasting to anyone who desires to fast and grow spiritually, in their sacrificial journey.

—Evangelist Charity Fisher, M.Div.

THE OTHER SIDE OF *Midnight*

A 21-Day Fasting Guide to Life Transformation

DR. ANGEL WHITE

THE OTHER SIDE OF MIDNIGHT
A 21-Day Fasting Guide to Life Transformation

Copyright © 2019 by Dr. Angel White
All rights reserved.

All rights reserved. This book is protected by the copyright laws of the United States of America. This book may not be copied or reprinted for commercial gain or profit. The use of quotations or occasional page copying for personal or group study is permitted and encouraged. Permission will be granted upon request.

Unless otherwise identified, Scripture quotations are from the King James Version. Copyright © 1982 by Thomas Nelson, Inc. Used by permission. All rights reserved.
reserved.

Final Step Publishing, LLC

PO Box 1441
Suffolk, VA 23439

For Worldwide Distribution. Printed in U.S.A.

Soft cover ISBN: 978-1-7335842-9-6
E-Book ISBN: 978-1-7337462-1-2

Library of Congress Number: 2019934639

Book Cover & Interior Design: Cooke Consulting & Creations

CONTENTS

Foreword	10
Preface	14
Week 1 Midnight Message	16
Day 1: The Oneness of God	19
Day 2: House	20
Day 3: Benefactor	21
Day 4: Door	22
Day 5: Behold	23
Week 2 Midnight Message	24
Day 6: Add To & Secure	27
Day 7: Harvest	28
Day 8: Wall	29
Day 9: Basket or Container	30
Day 10: Work and Praise	31
Week 3 Midnight Message	32
Day 11: Open Hand	35

Day 12: Shepherd's Staff   36

Day 13: Waters   37

Day 14: Continue   38

Day 15: Shield or Thorn   39

Week 4 Midnight Message   40

Day 16: Eye, Knowledge   43

Day 17: Speak   44

Day 18: Stronghold   45

Day 19: Sunrise, Time   46

Day 20: Head, Chief   47

Week 5 Midnight Message   48

Day 21: Eat, Teeth   51

Final Midnight Message   54

About the Author   57

FOREWORD

I was about 12 years old playing on the middle school basketball team—a young, skinny kid with a boxed haircut, sports glasses in an oversized sweat suit. Each day we had practice immediately after school at the same time. It would begin at 3:35 pm and end at 4:45 pm. I would stand outside of the gym watching friends load the bus and others jump into the cars of their parents who had arrived on time to pick them up. However, like a telephone pole cemented into the ground, I was still standing there. I was not on the bus nor had my ride arrived. I would stand there for what felt like hours waiting for my parent to show up. Staring at my navy-blue Guess watch wrapped around my left wrist and looking at the second-hand run laps around the watch bezel became a regular routine because being late had become his norm. Often in the cold of winter and with early sunsets, I would stand weary and literally in the dark just waiting for his headlights to shine around the corner.

This is when time really started to have true meaning for me. It was while standing in the frigid cold dark hole of life awaiting a ride home that I began understanding that time and timing were everything. If my father had come just 10 or 15 minutes earlier, I would be with peers, smiling and jovially jumping into his tan colored Volvo headed to McDonald's for a burger. His arrival 15-30 minutes late left me lonely only accompanied by my thoughts and concerns of just how long it was going to take for this trauma to dissipate. If he had come early things would be good, but late and it was awful. It was a matter of minutes that would determine my happiness or frustration. What a difference timing makes.

This childhood experience with time and timing are why this 21-day devotional with Dr. Angel White is so brilliant. She has performed the perfect marriage between time and timing. She shows up with great timing by providing a message at midnight then guides us for just the right time length in the number of days for transformation. The message at midnight is the most quintessential time to offer a weekly encouragement as it reminds us of how quickly life can change. In a matter of seconds, we are led from one day into the next. Starting the weekly motivations at 11:59 pm and ending somewhere into the 12 am morning of the next day was brilliant. We are catapulted from a long day of fatigue and worries over into a morning message that lifts our heads and causes us, like butterflies, to glide freely into an unknown future full of God's promises.

This devotional masterfully helps us constantly find refreshing and renewal as she speaks to us at the unique but ideal time of midnight. We start the conversation at midnight with a problem but end the conversation with hope. Midnight in imagery is a boring, brown, and gloomy green caterpillar being tightly swaddled in a dingy silk cocoon for a moment and then reemerging chrysalis as a pleasantly decorated purple, turquoise, white, and pink colored beautiful butterfly. This devotional will create that change in your life because it helps us experience God's power at midnight. Midnight is the time for true transformation. It was midnight when Paul and Silas prayed (Acts 16:25) causing the jailhouse doors to part open like the Red Sea, chains to be broken like an old 2012 Tasha Cobbs Leonard song, and a family to be saved like passengers crashing into the Hudson River on flight 1549. Midnight was the time God chose to strike down the first-born males of Egypt (Exodus 12:2) to prove that He alone controlled life then, and I believe that these devotionals remind us that He is still in control of our lives now. It is at midnight that we all experience that proverbial transition from weeping in the night (Proverbs 20:5) to joy in the morning. Finally, it is at midnight that Dr. Angel introduces us to the metaphorizing power of God to break us from our cocoons and release us into a brighter next day. This devotional will be the most empowering minute of your day. It reminds me of a poem by Dr. Benjamin Mays when he described, "God's Minute":

> "I have only just a minute, only sixty seconds in it. Forced upon me, can't refuse it. Didn't seek it, didn't choose it. But it's up to me to use. I must suffer if I lose it. Give account if I abuse it. Just a tiny little minute, but eternity is in it."

How's eternity looking for you? Will you take a minute for the next 21 days and reach the other side of midnight? Have you been standing in any dark or frigid cold moments waiting for your ride of life to pick you up but it feels as if you have been forgotten? Or maybe, you have been staring at a situation watch that only leaves you feeling like a second hand going around in circles. These next few pages are filled with TIMELY insights to help you maximize your future in a short TIME period of only 21 days. I earlier complained that my father would pick me up late, but there is one fact I failed to mention. He did not come when I wanted him to come, but he always picked me up. Always. Turning these next few pages of this book and experiencing God's voice through Dr. Angel are a reminder that even when God, our Father, does not show up in the timeliest fashion according to our preference, He will always pick you up. This devotional book is an after-midnight morning "pick you up." Welcome to the other side of midnight!

Dr. Dwight S Riddick, II

PREFACE

Let me just take a moment and help you understand how this book is to be understood. It is indeed a 21-day devotional journey. However, each week begins with an encouraging word that is designed to be read at midnight on Sunday going into Monday. Then each day of that week will follow as a short 1-minute devotional to inspire you throughout the day. The devotional takes us through Psalm 119 that is as unique as me asking you to read at midnight. This Psalm strategically has 22 segments with each having 8 verses opening with the Hebrew Alphabet. I have attempted to bring revelation not only from the scriptures but also from the words represented by each letter. Each day gives new light for our lives and a fresh perspective into God's word. You choose your particular Fast (what you will yield to God over the next 21 days: for example, The Daniel Fast). Then here you will get your prayer focus.

Midnight is really interesting. I love midnight because the house is quiet and you can get some things done that you weren't able to get done during the day. However, the downside of midnight is that when the house is quiet you can think of some things that would otherwise distract you or have you not being positive. So, to keep us in a positive lane, I just wanted to send out a couple of messages at midnight. Let's get started.

Week 1: Midnight Message
STATUS UPDATE

A couple of months ago, my children and I went on vacation and while we were there my daughter lost a very expensive set of headphones. I won't tell you the brand, but she lost them. And when she lost them, she was upset and so was I. I called the hotel and I asked them. I said, "You know umm, we lost a set of headphones. We're pretty sure where we left them. We remember the last place we saw them. Can you help us out?" The hotel representative said, "Fill out a claim; we'll open a case. Describe the headphones, and after you describe them and your case, we'll start looking for them. We'll give it about 14-15 days and send you a status update. Then we'll give it another couple of days and then we'll send you what we found. If we haven't found it within 20 days or so, we will send you an email to let you know."

So, that's what they did. They sent me a status update and an email stating that unfortunately they haven't been able to find the headphones, so at this point, we have to close the case. Of course, I was upset because I wanted the headphones to be found and we haven't found them yet. But here's the revelation I received. Let's look at Philippians 3:13-14. I have my big coffee table Bible for you, I have my prayer cloth for you, and I have my midnight pillow for you. Are you ready? Okay. Philippians 3:13-14 it says "Brethren, I count not myself to have apprehended: but this one thing I do, forgetting those things which are behind, and reaching forth unto those things which are before, I press toward the mark for the prize of the high calling of God in Christ Jesus." At my grandmother's church, they would say, read it again! "But

Brethren, I count not myself to have apprehended: but this one thing I do, forgetting those things which are behind, and reaching forth unto those things which are before, I press toward the mark for the prize of the high calling of God in Christ Jesus."

So, here it is. I want to ask you tonight: when was the last time you did a status update? When was the last time you looked at your life and did a real-life status update? This revelation messed me up. I wanted the headphones to be found. I wanted them to give me a good report and say, "Hey, we have your headphones." But this is what they did: they gave me a window of time for them to be found, then they gave me another window of time for them to keep looking for them. And then they gave me a time frame of when they would give me the status update. I think in our lives we have to give ourselves permission to do a status update. We must give ourselves permission to find a window of time to say, "Okay, this is what I've lost." And I'm not talking about grief; grief has its own cycle.

I am not going to minimize the opportunities that we need to really deal with our losses. However, there are some things like headphones, there are some things that are a little more lightweight than others. But we spend a lot of our time on it. Too much time. We spend our midnights dwelling on it. But I want to tell you that maybe it's time for all of us to do a status update. To say, you know what, it's been 30 days, it's been a year, and I'm still dealing with the same stuff. It's been 2 years, I think it's time for us to do a status update. I think it's time for us to say I was looking for it, I gave myself time, continued to search for it, and gave myself additional time. But unfortunately, this was something that I lost, or this was something that I didn't succeed in, or this was a goal that I didn't meet. And it's okay. Because now I'm doing a status update, and the status update taught me this: we just have to go buy some more headphones.

And, so, the status update on our life may teach us that now is the time for us to move on. How do we have this confirmation? The confirmation is this: it's found in Philippians 3:13-14. In order for us to press, we have to forget what's behind; we have to start reaching forward. We can't keep hiding behind some things. Sometimes it's time to do a status update and case closed. I am done, and it's time to move on.

"The Oneness of God"
ALEPH (Hebrew)

Blessed are the undefiled in the way, who walk in the law of the LORD. ² Blessed are they that keep his testimonies, and that seek him with the whole heart. ³ They also do no iniquity: they walk in his ways. ⁴ Thou hast commanded us to keep thy precepts diligently. ⁵ O that my ways were directed to keep thy statutes! ⁶ Then shall I not be ashamed, when I have respect unto all thy commandments. ⁷ I will praise thee with uprightness of heart, when I shall have learned thy righteous judgments. ⁸ I will keep thy statutes: O forsake me not utterly.

Psalm 119:1-8

Do you know that you're worthy of His favor? Open the year with intentional efforts to draw closer to God. Press into His presence daily, and you'll see the goodness of the Lord. Today we put away past shame and past disappointments, and we celebrate the God who's seen us through it all. Walk in God's strength today!

_____
_____
_____
_____
_____
_____
_____
_____

"House"
BETH (Hebrew)

⁹ Wherewithal shall a young man cleanse his way? by taking heed thereto according to thy word. ¹⁰ With my whole heart have I sought thee: O let me not wander from thy commandments. ¹¹ Thy word have I hid in mine heart, that I might not sin against thee. ¹² Blessed art thou, O Lord: teach me thy statutes. ¹³ With my lips have I declared all the judgments of thy mouth. ¹⁴ I have rejoiced in the way of thy testimonies, as much as in all riches. ¹⁵ I will meditate in thy precepts, and have respect unto thy ways. ¹⁶ I will delight myself in thy statutes: I will not forget thy word.

Psalm 119:9-16

Do you know that God wants to bless and restore the power in your house? Fasting is a cleanse both physically and spiritually. Fasting deals with our heart and home. Over the years, our hopes and dreams can become depleted. Today speak life back into your house. Yes! We declare: "Love, life, laughter, joy, salvation, peace, health, and prosperity . . . in our house." This is relevant for your house (physical home, the church, and your body). Pray for God to refill your house with His glory. Remember, your personal fast is a physical sacrifice, making supernatural deposits that will pay off in your future. Here we Go!

_____

_____

_____

_____

_____

_____

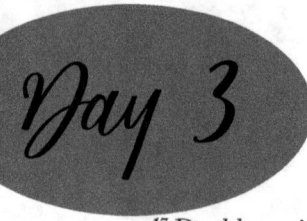

"Benefactor"
GIMEL (Hebrew)

[17] Deal bountifully with thy servant, that I may live, and keep thy word. [18] Open thou mine eyes, that I may behold wondrous things out of thy law. [19] I am a stranger in the earth: hide not thy commandments from me. [20] My soul breaketh for the longing that it hath unto thy judgments at all times. [21] Thou hast rebuked the proud that are cursed, which do err from thy commandments. [22] Remove from me reproach and contempt; for I have kept thy testimonies. [23] Princes also did sit and speak against me: but thy servant did meditate in thy statutes. [24] Thy testimonies also are my delight and my counselors.

Psalm 119:17-24

God deal with us bountifully, let us see your wonders, and rebuke the proud as we meditate on your statutes. Simply put, "God is our help." Today, we focus on our "God Supply." These are the things that we know only God can do. He is our benefactor: supporter, helper, provider, and partner. Allow yourself to expand your vision today. Don't think small. The first few days of fasting make you feel a little weary, but press in. Delight in the Lord as you believe Him for greater. It's worth the hunger pains and delayed craving. What we are believing God for is beyond our ability. Only He can supply this, manifest this, and allow us the privilege of enjoying the breakthrough. (Read Psalm 37:4-5.) Here we Go!

"Door"
DALETH (Hebrew)

25 My soul cleaveth unto the dust: quicken thou me according to thy word. 26 I have declared my ways, and thou heardest me: teach me thy statutes. 27 Make me to understand the way of thy precepts: so shall I talk of thy wondrous works. 28 My soul melteth for heaviness: strengthen thou me according unto thy word. 29 Remove from me the way of lying: and grant me thy law graciously. 30 I have chosen the way of truth: thy judgments have I laid before me. 31 I have stuck unto thy testimonies: O LORD, put me not to shame. 32 I will run the way of thy commandments, when thou shalt enlarge my heart.

Psalm 119:25-32

Celebrating open doors today with a challenge . . .all the doors are not physical. This text celebrates choosing the "way" of truth. It speaks of an open understanding of God's word and a heart that is open to being loved by God. God is setting before us open doors of opportunity; however, we have to be ready to walk through them. This next level of greatness requires us to choose doors that lead to our wholeness, our peace, and our personal revival. We can't afford to walk through the door excited but unprepared. God, thank you that all doors are opening that you have ordained for us. When we go forth this time we go in the fullness of God: Peace, Prudence, and Power. Prosperity will be the result of our Preparation. Here we Go!

_____

_____

_____

_____

"Behold"
HE (Hebrew)

33 Teach me, O LORD, the way of thy statutes; and I shall keep it unto the end. 34 Give me understanding, and I shall keep thy law; yea, I shall observe it with my whole heart. 35 Make me to go in the path of thy commandments; for therein do I delight. 36 Incline my heart unto thy testimonies, and not to covetousness. 37 Turn away mine eyes from beholding vanity; and quicken thou me in thy way. 38 Stablish thy word unto thy servant, who is devoted to thy fear. 39 Turn away my reproach which I fear: for thy judgments are good. 40 Behold, I have longed after thy precepts: quicken me in thy righteousness.

Psalm 119:33-40

God is about to show off! Fasting opens up your heart to receive the revelation of God. We need God to move in a miraculous way. Just a glimpse of the possibilities. A preview of coming attractions. "If we ever needed the Lord before, we sure do need him now!" As we observe His word and make it our delight (verse 34-35), he shows us the way of righteousness. This Psalm repeatedly requests for God to teach, reveal, and revive. Give way to the revelation! When we 'Behold,' it means to become in awe of God. He's about to give us a jaw-dropping, awe-struck revelation. Today, we look for our God moments. Here we Go!

Week 2: Midnight Message
A PLAY DOUGH TESTIMONY

Greetings night owls, here we go again. We are up and it's midnight. Here we go. I have my glasses on to cover up the fact I don't have on any makeup. I have my prayer shawl on. I have my big coffee table Bible, and I have my pillow. We are ready to just have a moment at midnight. I told you before that midnight is the time the house is quiet and you can receive a word from the Lord, but midnight can also be a time when you are distracted and distressed over things. So, to turn that thing around, I want to offer a message at midnight just to encourage your heart and encourage your soul right before you finally lay down and go to sleep.

So, I don't know if it's because I'm a parent or whether I just see things differently, but tonight we're going to talk about a play dough testimony. You know, play dough, that comes in little colorful containers. You played with it as a child—you mushed it up and you put it back in the container. And then sometimes your parents or your grandparents would yell at you because you'd have little pieces of it everywhere. Or you would leave it out of the container, and it would get extremely hard and you had to throw it away.

So, we're going to talk for just a few moments about a play dough testimony. Where does the revelation come from? Are you ready? Do you have your Bible? Let's look at 2 Corinthians 4:8-10. It says, "We are troubled on every side, yet not distressed; we are perplexed, but not in despair; Persecuted, but not forsaken; cast down, but not destroyed; Always bearing about in the body the dying of the Lord Jesus, that the life also of Jesus might be made manifest in our body." Did you read it? Let's read it again. It says, "We are troubled on every side, yet not distressed; we are perplexed, but not in despair; Persecuted, but not forsaken; cast down, but not destroyed; Always bearing about in the body the dying of the Lord Jesus, that the life also of Jesus might be made manifest in our body".

A play dough testimony. This is the way it goes. I was thinking about it when I began to read this scripture because it gives us so much power to understand that we can go through so much and yet make it out on the other end. So, when we begin to think about 2 Corinthians 4:8-10, it says this is what we go through, all of us go through something. We are hard pressed, we are perplexed, we are crushed, but we are not forsaken. Here's the play dough testimony. You and I have to be more like play dough. When you start thinking about play dough, kids take it out of the container, they crush it, they form it into everything, they pound on it, they try to do everything they can to manipulate that play dough. But at the end of the day, it's still somehow maintains this blob-like form because that's what it was created to be.

So, I want to tell you this. Many of us have to be more like play dough when it comes to life. Even though there are things that come to try and crush us, try to manipulate who we are, and try to form us into something that we weren't really created to be, we must remain like the play dough. And when you have a child who really cares about their play dough, after they are done playing, they place it back into its container. And then its sealed up. If the play dough is put back into its container and place the lid on top, the next time the child has an opportunity to play with it, the play dough is refreshed. However, if the play dough is not put back into its container and sealed up, it's hard, it's flaky, and it's of use to no one.

Check this out. A lot of times we go through being hard pressed, we go through being crushed, we go through being perplexed, we go through being persecuted, we go through being destroyed, but this is what we have to remember. We allow all those things to happen to us and we forget that at the end of the day, we have to go back in our container, which is Jesus Christ. We have to allow the lid of His love and His power to be put back on us so that way we can be refreshed and then we can start anew another day. But if we don't do that, we allow ourselves to stay out, to be exposed, to get hard, and to get flaky, and we're of use to no one.

Have a play dough testimony that no matter what you go through, go back in your container. No matter what life brings to you, no matter how people try to form you, no matter how people try to manipulate you, no matter how you've gone through being persecuted, perplexed, hard pressed, always go back to Jesus. Remember, we are not forsaken, and remember verse 10. It says we have always to carry around in our body the dying of the Lord Jesus that the life of Jesus also may be manifested in our body. How do we manifest that? Jesus got up after everything He went through. How do I manifest that in my body? After going through whatever you have to go through you still have to get up. Why? Because Jesus lives in you.

"Add To & Secure"
WAW (Hebrew)

> *⁴¹ Let thy mercies come also unto me, O Lord, even thy salvation, according to thy word. ⁴² So shall I have wherewith to answer him that reproacheth me: for I trust in thy word. ⁴³ And take not the word of truth utterly out of my mouth; for I have hoped in thy judgments. ⁴⁴ So shall I keep thy law continually for ever and ever. ⁴⁵ And I will walk at liberty: for I seek thy precepts. ⁴⁶ I will speak of thy testimonies also before kings, and will not be ashamed. ⁴⁷ And I will delight myself in thy commandments, which I have loved. ⁴⁸ My hands also will I lift up unto thy commandments, which I have loved; and I will meditate in thy statutes.*
>
> **Psalm 119:41-48**

It's Inventory time! Take stock of what you have. Does it empower you? Does it draw you closer to God? Does it increase your love for self and others? If you have more spiritual subtractions than additions, it's time to call somethings forth. The opening verse declares "Let your mercies come also to me." This Psalm is about falling in love with God's word and the power to overcome adversity by calling out what one needs. When was the last time you asked God for some additions? God add to me: love, grace, mercy, health, healing, and wisdom. Restore unto me: joy, laughter, dancing, and singing. When fasting, it's easy to focus only on what we're giving up, but today call forth the things you need that food can't supply. Here we Go!

_____

_____

_____

_____

_____

"Harvest"
ZAYIN (Hebrew)

⁴⁹ Remember the word unto thy servant, upon which thou hast caused me to hope. ⁵⁰ This is my comfort in my affliction: for thy word hath quickened me. ⁵¹ The proud have had me greatly in derision: yet have I not declined from thy law. ⁵² I remembered thy judgments of old, O LORD; and have comforted myself. ⁵³ Horror hath taken hold upon me because of the wicked that forsake thy law. ⁵⁴ Thy statutes have been my songs in the house of my pilgrimage. ⁵⁵ I have remembered thy name, O LORD, in the night, and have kept thy law. ⁵⁶ This I had, because I kept thy precepts.

Psalm 119:49-56

You have caused me to hope (verse 49). Your Word has given me life (verse 50). Did we think the term "giving me life" came only from the Urban Dictionary? The psalmist declared it first! Simply put, God's Word makes me excited; His promises give me hope and comfort. This text is "giving me life" right now. I know that our harvest is coming! God is going to remember every seed planted. When we prayed and our tears became our food. When we sowed financially and didn't really have it to give. When we gave time to others that we needed for ourselves. God remembers! Get ready! God is about to release blessings that we forgot we even asked for. Press in. Stay the course. Here we Go!

_____

_____

_____

_____

_____

"Wall"
HETH (Hebrew)

⁵⁷ Thou art my portion, O LORD: I have said that I would keep thy words. ⁵⁸ I intreated thy favour with my whole heart: be merciful unto me according to thy word. ⁵⁹ I thought on my ways, and turned my feet unto thy testimonies. ⁶⁰ I made haste, and delayed not to keep thy commandments. ⁶¹ The bands of the wicked have robbed me: but I have not forgotten thy law. ⁶² At midnight I will rise to give thanks unto thee because of thy righteous judgments. ⁶³ I am a companion of all them that fear thee, and of them that keep thy precepts. ⁶⁴ The earth, O LORD, is full of thy mercy: teach me thy statutes.

Psalm 119:57-64

Walls usually get a bad rap, but not today. This "wall" in Hebrew is not to block us, but it's to protect us. Today we pray for God's protection. This protection covers us from the elements. God is our wall of protection. Today we yield to the full knowledge of God and His ability to protect and guide us. The psalmist declared, "I thought about my ways, and turned my feet toward you" (verse 59). He also declared "I intreated your favor with my whole heart" (verse 58). In short: God, I no longer want what I desire. I want what You have for me because it's so much better. God's blessings are already sealed and protected by His word. Today we decree that we want what God wants. He protects us, provides for us, and His favor will push us into our destiny! Here we Go!

_____

_____

_____

_____

_____

_____

"Basket or Container"
TETH (Hebrew)

⁶⁵ *Thou hast dealt well with thy servant, O LORD, according unto thy word.* ⁶⁶ *Teach me good judgment and knowledge: for I have believed thy commandments.* ⁶⁷ *Before I was afflicted I went astray: but now have I kept thy word.* ⁶⁸ *Thou art good, and doest good; teach me thy statutes.* ⁶⁹ *The proud have forged a lie against me: but I will keep thy precepts with my whole heart.* ⁷⁰ *Their heart is as fat as grease; but I delight in thy law.* ⁷¹ *It is good for me that I have been afflicted; that I might learn thy statutes.* ⁷² *The law of thy mouth is better unto me than thousands of gold and silver.*

Psalm 119:65-72

How big is your basket? The Hebrews would use baskets to catch fish or to store food or tools. The basket is a symbol of blessings. "Your basket and your kneading bowl will be blessed" (Deuteronomy 28:5). I realize that many times I've been fishing with a small basket only expecting the minimum, just getting by, just surviving the day. This is not the expectation we should have. Get a bigger basket! If you want more you must toss those low expectations and reach for the biggest container you have; one so big you can't handle it alone. Get ready for the outpouring! "You have dealt well with Your servant" (verse 65). The word "well" in the text means bountifully. Today we change the size of our baskets. Pray bigger, think broader, and desire God's best. Here we Go!

_____

_____

_____

_____

_____

"Work and Praise"
YOD (Hebrew)

⁷³ Thy hands have made me and fashioned me: give me understanding, that I may learn thy commandments. ⁷⁴ They that fear thee will be glad when they see me; because I have hoped in thy word. ⁷⁵ I know, O LORD, that thy judgments are right, and that thou in faithfulness hast afflicted me. ⁷⁶ Let, I pray thee, thy merciful kindness be for my comfort, according to thy word unto thy servant. ⁷⁷ Let thy tender mercies come unto me, that I may live: for thy law is my delight. ⁷⁸ Let the proud be ashamed; for they dealt perversely with me without a cause: but I will meditate in thy precepts. ⁷⁹ Let those that fear thee turn unto me, and those that have known thy testimonies. ⁸⁰ Let my heart be sound in thy statutes; that I be not ashamed.

Psalm 119:73-80

Do you still have your praise? It's been 10 days! We're about halfway there. It's already been a journey, but this is the time when we all need a little push to keep going. SHARE YOUR PROGRESS, PRAISE REPORTS, or RECIPES. Share how things are going for you so we can encourage each other. The psalmist continues to recall the great mercies of God and His precepts. The core of the text is to love God's commandments and find comfort in His word. Fasting is a discipline resulting in great benefits. Fasting breaks the spirit of delay and pushes us forward into our destiny. Keep going forward! Here we Go!

_____

_____

_____

_____

_____

_____

WEEK 3: Midnight Message
ARE YOU A WINDOW WASHER?

Greetings night owls, here we are, once again. And its 12 midnight. I am excited to offer another piece to a message at midnight. But again, this is the time everything is still, it's quiet, you can get a good revelation right before you go to bed. And then it's also the opportunity for us to do some introspection and recap our day. You know what? No matter what sort of day you had, you made it. Now it's time to reflect, get a good word from God, and snuggle up and go to sleep. So, here I am, with my big Bible, I have my pillow and my prayer cloth, so I'm ready. So, let's begin.

I had the opportunity to take an amazing cruise with two great preacher friends of mine. They are amazing; they are my lifetime friends. But I was terrified because I had never been on a cruise before. I've flown so many places, but I've always been a little bit apprehensive about taking a cruise. But they convinced me, and I went. It was the best decision ever—my children loved it and, we had a blast. But this was the thing. One morning I woke up really early and I went on the lido deck. Don't judge me, but that's where all the food is. I was there so early that I was waiting for the buffet to open (pray for me). While waiting, I saw this woman working and she was washing the windows. So, tonight, I want to talk to you about window washing.

While she was washing the windows, everybody was just walking by her (there were other people waiting for the buffet as well). She was just working so diligently. She was so intricate in every detail that she made, to make sure that all of the windows on that side of the ship were clean. And as she was cleaning, people walked by her several times. Nobody seemed to notice what she was doing, but for some reason, it just stood out to me that she was washing those windows. And while I was watching her washing those windows, it made me want to go outside. Now, I'm telling you, I was terrified of the cruise. But it made me want to go outside to the top deck. So, I did, and I sat there and I watched her wash these windows.

All of a sudden, it came to me. A lot of times, we always think that washing windows is like the minimal; it's the bottom of the totem pole. Nobody wants to wash windows. You hire a maid and they may say they will wash clothes and wash dishes, but they don't do windows. But here's the revelation. Everybody needs somebody who'll do windows. Are you a window washer? Are you somebody that helps other people see clearly? When was the last time you washed windows? Let's look at Proverbs 29. Proverbs 29:18 says, "Where there is no vision the people perish. But he that keepeth the law, happy is he."

When was the last time you washed windows? Everybody has to have a vision. Everybody has to see. People walked past this young lady over and over again. Nobody noticed her and she almost didn't notice anybody. But I noticed in that moment that without her on that ship, the windows would have handprints on them. Without her on that ship, the windows would have spots on them and nobody would want to walk outside. Nobody would be able to see the beauty of those sunsets or the beauty of the ocean itself. All because the windows were dirty. She was helping us on that ship to have vision.

Who are you helping to have vision? I know the job seems like it's at the bottom of the totem pole, the job may not seem glamorous, and it may seem like people are not listening to you. But keep making people see the vision that God has given you. Keep washing those windows. Because if you don't keep washing the windows of your spirit, if you don't keep washing the windows of your ministry, of your household, and of your family, and if you don't keep washing the windows and keep casting a new vision, then all you'll have is a life that's full of other people's handprints. Just imagine, you can't see me. That's what it's like when other people have put their stamps and their handprints all over your vision—others can't see.

Keep washing those windows because the Bible declares that without vision people perish. Keep doing what you're doing. Keep casting that vision because happy is he that keeps the law. You stick with it and you'll be happy. It'll pay off. At the end of the day when I was watching that young lady washing those windows, I went up to her, and I said, "Thank you so much for making this ship so beautiful. I've had a wonderful time and it's because of you." She replied, "Thank you. I said, "Do you know that your job matters because without you people can't see out here." As she stood there, her face lit up and she said, "Thank you so much."

And I want to tell you today—I don't know if anybody has told you lately—but I love you. I want to tell you that your job matters. Who you are matters, and if you just keep it up and if you stick with it, you're helping someone to see clearly. Keep washing those windows. Keep at the hard work because your vision is going to pay off.

"Open Hand"
KAPH (Hebrew)

⁸¹ My soul fainteth for thy salvation: but I hope in thy word. ⁸² Mine eyes fail for thy word, saying, When wilt thou comfort me? ⁸³ For I am become like a bottle in the smoke; yet do I not forget thy statutes. ⁸⁴ How many are the days of thy servant? when wilt thou execute judgment on them that persecute me? ⁸⁵ The proud have digged pits for me, which are not after thy law. ⁸⁶ All thy commandments are faithful: they persecute me wrongfully; help thou me. ⁸⁷ They had almost consumed me upon earth; but I forsook not thy precepts. ⁸⁸ Quicken me after thy lovingkindness; so shall I keep the testimony of thy mouth.

Psalm 119:81-88

"The hand of God is able to provide favor and justice." We often seek the hand of God only for the manifestation of material things. The psalmist has now moved to an active plea to ask God for justice. Day 10 was the hand that comforts. Day 11 is the hand that serves justice. "All your commandments are faithful; they persecute me wrongly; help thou me." (verse 86). Is there anyone that needs justice, order, and for God to arise on your behalf? Today we stop fighting our own battles and we call upon Jehovah-Nissi (God our Banner); the God who fights for us. Simply put: let go and let God. Here we Go!

"Shepherd's Staff"
LAMED (Hebrew)

⁸⁹ For ever, O LORD, thy word is settled in heaven. ⁹⁰ Thy faithfulness is unto all generations: thou hast established the earth, and it abideth. ⁹¹ They continue this day according to thine ordinances: for all are thy servants. ⁹² Unless thy law had been my delights, I should then have perished in mine affliction. ⁹³ I will never forget thy precepts: for with them thou hast quickened me. ⁹⁴ I am thine, save me: for I have sought thy precepts. ⁹⁵ The wicked have waited for me to destroy me: but I will consider thy testimonies. ⁹⁶ I have seen an end of all perfection: but thy commandment is exceeding broad.

Psalm 119:89-96

Today we pray for guidance and leadership. We lean on God's authority today. His word has already been established in the heavens and on earth. Thank you, God: "Your word is settled, your faithfulness endures, and you've ordained our path" (verses 89-91). Isn't it good to know that our God is our guide, our true example of leadership? Our prayers are with all government employees and praying for God's sustainable power and breakthrough. Takeover Great Shepherd! Show off Great God! The government is upon your shoulders, Jesus (Isaiah 9:6). Here we Go!

_____

_____

_____

_____

_____

_____

Day 13

"Waters"
MEM (Hebrew)

⁹⁷ O how love I thy law! it is my meditation all the day. ⁹⁸ Thou through thy commandments hast made me wiser than mine enemies: for they are ever with me. ⁹⁹ I have more understanding than all my teachers: for thy testimonies are my meditation. ¹⁰⁰ I understand more than the ancients, because I keep thy precepts. ¹⁰¹ I have refrained my feet from every evil way, that I might keep thy word. ¹⁰² I have not departed from thy judgments: for thou hast taught me. ¹⁰³ How sweet are thy words unto my taste! yea, sweeter than honey to my mouth! ¹⁰⁴ Through thy precepts I get understanding: therefore I hate every false way.

Psalm 119:97-104

We fast to seek understanding, direction, and wisdom in a chaotic world. The 13th letter of the Hebrew Alphabet symbolizes trusting God during the unknown storms of life. The psalmist encourages himself: When my enemies rise up to speak against me, I remember your word; a word sweeter than honey in my mouth (verses 98, 103). Don't allow chaos to get you off track, steal your joy, or make you frustrated. Today, speak life. Be careful with your words. Allow them to become living waters (Proverbs 18:4). Keep pressing in. Here we Go!

"Continue"
NUN (Hebrew)

¹⁰⁵ Thy word is a lamp unto my feet, and a light unto my path. ¹⁰⁶ I have sworn, and I will perform it, that I will keep thy righteous judgments. ¹⁰⁷ I am afflicted very much: quicken me, O LORD, according unto thy word. ¹⁰⁸ Accept, I beseech thee, the freewill offerings of my mouth, O LORD, and teach me thy judgments. ¹⁰⁹ My soul is continually in my hand: yet do I not forget thy law. ¹¹⁰ The wicked have laid a snare for me: yet I erred not from thy precepts. ¹¹¹ Thy testimonies have I taken as an heritage for ever: for they are the rejoicing of my heart. ¹¹² I have inclined mine heart to perform thy statutes alway, even unto the end.

Psalm 119:105-112

Keep moving forward. God has already given us the flashlight, so let's take the voyage. "Your word is a lamp to my feet and a light to my path" (verse 105). Get ready to move forward today; no looking back, no souvenirs, and no regrets. There are 7 days left to our 21-day journey. Your press and your push is not in vain. Fast for results this week. Lock in on the things you're believing God for. Remember His faithfulness to NUN (meaning all generations; a continued legacy of greatness). This Fast includes generational blessings, not just temporary fixes. We pray for blessings that continue. Keep Moving Forward! Here we Go!

_____

_____

_____

_____

_____

_____

Day 15

"Shield or Thorn"
SAMEK (Hebrew)

> *¹¹³ I hate vain thoughts: but thy law do I love. ¹¹⁴ Thou art my hiding place and my shield: I hope in thy word. ¹¹⁵ Depart from me, ye evildoers: for I will keep the commandments of my God. ¹¹⁶ Uphold me according unto thy word, that I may live: and let me not be ashamed of my hope. ¹¹⁷ Hold thou me up, and I shall be safe: and I will have respect unto thy statutes continually. ¹¹⁸ Thou hast trodden down all them that err from thy statutes: for their deceit is falsehood. ¹¹⁹ Thou puttest away all the wicked of the earth like dross: therefore I love thy testimonies. ¹²⁰ My flesh trembleth for fear of thee; and I am afraid of thy judgments.*

Psalm 119:113-120

Thorns are not created to hurt the rose but to protect it. God has us enclosed like a shield of thorns on a rose. "You are my hiding place and my shield; I hope in your word" (verse 114). Today, we rest in our hiding place. When playing the childhood game, "hide & go, seek," a good hiding place is where you almost fall asleep while the game is going on because they can't find you. It's the same today. We have a great hiding place in God so we can rest and relax where the enemy can't find us (verse 115). Flex your shield today (Ephesians 6:16). Here we Go!

Week 4: Midnight Message
Adventures of A Hot Air Balloon

Greetings night owls, thank you so much for hanging out and for staying up late. Remember, this is our time: the whole house is quiet and there's not a lot going on. This is our time to refuel, to recharge after a long day, and to just have a moment with the Lord. I'm glad that we can share this moment together.

    I have my prayer cloth and Bible, and I have a message at midnight that I would like to share with you. Are you ready? Let's go. Tonight, I want to talk about the adventures of a hot air balloon. As scared as I am of a lot a little stuff, I want to tell you about the time I was serious about getting in a hot air balloon. I began to read up on hot air balloons and what you need to take with you in order to be prepared. It came to my surprise that there are a lot of instructions. There is a list of things you should bring and how you should dress. And I want to tell you, I haven't taken that trip yet but to read up on what you need to bring really blessed my soul, and so I just want to be able to share that with you. And so, if you are preparing yourself to do what you've never done before, if you are preparing yourself to take an adventure that you've never taken before, to believe God to take you to heights that you've never been before, I want to tell you that the instructions that you need to take a hot air balloon trip are almost the same instructions that you need to prepare yourself for this next great level in God.

    Listen, they tell you to make sure that you dress in layers, make sure that you cover up your feet (don't wear flip flops or any shoes where your toes aren't covered). You are also instructed to wear a hat (especially if you are tall) because inside of the hot air balloon it gets hot, and the higher you go, the hotter it gets. They also tell you to bring only the essential items with you because it's a tight space. Finally, they tell you to bring a camera.

So, whenever we are ready to do great things in God, to take this next leap, to take this next great step, or whatever that adventure may be, we may need to follow the instructions as if we're about to take a hot air balloon trip. Why? Here's the revelation. In Esther 2:15 it reads, "Now with the time came for Esther, the daughter of Abihail the uncle of Mordecai who had taken her as his daughter, to go into the King, she requested nothing but what Haggai, the King's eunuch, the custodian of the women had advised. And Esther obtained favor in the side of all who saw her." Haggai told Esther to only take what's necessary. Esther went through one whole year of preparation, but when it was her time to go in to the King, when it was her turn to be elevated, when it was her turn to go a little higher, she took only what was necessary, only what Haggai had advised. And when she took it, she found favor with the King.

I want to tell you that sometimes when we are excited about elevation or about going to that next level in God and we get a glimpse of our future, we start trying to take a whole lot of people with us, we start to trying to grab a whole lot of things —we are simply doing too much. All of a sudden, we're trying to gather up things for ourselves. But hear me, maybe what we need to do is just take the essentials with us. Maybe like Esther we need to make sure we've been advised well. Who's advising your spirit? Who's advising you on this journey? Esther had Haggai to tell her not to be like all the other girls; that she didn't need all the other stuff, and to take only what Haggai told her.

Maybe we need to be a little like Esther and only take what's been advised. Maybe we need to be like the adventure of a hot air balloon when we get ready to go. We need to make sure that when we go we're dressed in layers. We need to make sure that, we're covered in prayer; that we're covered in God's blessings. We need to make sure that when we go that our feet are covered—that we have on the whole armor of God. When we go, we're not just going any kind of way but we've already been ordered, our steps have already been anointed by God, and our feet are even covered. When we go, just like on a hot air balloon, we need to make sure we have our cap on—that our head and mind is already prepared. But then along with that we understand that when you get ready for elevation, when you get ready to go up a little bit higher, you just might be in tight spaces.

It may not be easy, but your next level, this next great thing that God is about to do through you, may require you to be in tight spaces like on a hot air balloon. You can only take the essentials with you. You can't bring a picnic basket or invite all of your cousins. Everyone cannot go with you because it's a tight space.

And then the final instruction for going up in a hot air balloon is to take a camera. Everyone won't be able to go with you and experience the journey as you're experiencing, so a camera is necessary. Take pictures because what God is doing is awesome, and you have to come back and tell your story to others. Tell them God is real. His love is amazing, and only He could do this.

The Bible says that after Esther listened to Haggai, after she did what he advised her, she found favor in the sight of everybody who saw her. Listen, God is going to show you favor in front of everybody who sees you. Get ready, the hot air balloon is waiting; make sure you have everything with you.

 "Eye, Knowledge"
AYIN (Hebrew)

*¹²¹ I have done judgment and justice: leave me not to mine oppressors. ¹²² Be surety for thy servant for good: let not the proud oppress me. ¹²³ Mine eyes fail for thy salvation, and for the word of thy righteousness. ¹²⁴ Deal with thy servant according unto thy mercy, and teach me thy statutes. ¹²⁵ I am thy servant; give me understanding, that I may know thy testimonies. ¹²⁶ It is time for thee, L*ORD*, to work: for they have made void thy law. ¹²⁷ Therefore I love thy commandments above gold; yea, above fine gold. ¹²⁸ Therefore I esteem all thy precepts concerning all things to be right; and I hate every false way.*

Psalm 119:121-128

Today, we focus on gaining clarity and knowledge. The eye in this text represents a full understanding and insight. Where do you need clarity? Where do you need instruction? God's will is so much better than anything we could imagine. "Therefore, I love Your commandments more than gold, yes, than fine gold!" (verse 127) Gaining clarity gives us a "wealth" of knowledge. God giving us clarity is a real blessing. "The Blessings of the Lord makes one rich and adds no sorrow" (Proverbs 10:22). Seek Clarity Today & Enjoy God's Goodness. Here we Go!

"Speak"
PE (Hebrew)

¹²⁹ Thy testimonies are wonderful: therefore doth my soul keep them. ¹³⁰ The entrance of thy words giveth light; it giveth understanding unto the simple. ¹³¹ I opened my mouth, and panted: for I longed for thy commandments. ¹³² Look thou upon me, and be merciful unto me, as thou usest to do unto those that love thy name. ¹³³ Order my steps in thy word: and let not any iniquity have dominion over me. ¹³⁴ Deliver me from the oppression of man: so will I keep thy precepts. ¹³⁵ Make thy face to shine upon thy servant; and teach me thy statutes. ¹³⁶ Rivers of waters run down mine eyes, because they keep not thy law.

Psalm 119:129-136

Have you been quiet for too long? Your voice matters. Your words have power and influence. Speak it! Say it out loud! What do you see? What are you believing God for? Today we focus on opening our mouth in agreement with God's will and receiving favor. Speak to physical pain, "I am healed." Speak to emotional stress, "I have peace." Speak to financial lack, "I am set free." Send your glory God! The enemy seeks control over our destiny, but we declare, "Let God arise and our enemies be scattered" (Psalm 68:1). "The blessings of the Lord will overtake us (Deuteronomy. 28:2)." Speak it! Here we Go!

_____
_____
_____
_____
_____
_____
_____

"Stronghold"
TSADDE (Hebrew)

¹³⁷ Righteous art thou, O LORD, and upright are thy judgments. ¹³⁸ Thy testimonies that thou hast commanded are righteous and very faithful. ¹³⁹ My zeal hath consumed me, because mine enemies have forgotten thy words. ¹⁴⁰ Thy word is very pure: therefore thy servant loveth it. ¹⁴¹ I am small and despised: yet do not I forget thy precepts. ¹⁴² Thy righteousness is an everlasting righteousness, and thy law is the truth. ¹⁴³ Trouble and anguish have taken hold on me: yet thy commandments are my delights. ¹⁴⁴ The righteousness of thy testimonies is everlasting: give me understanding, and I shall live.

Psalm 119:137-144

Strongholds are defined in two ways: 1) the strongholds set up as traps during a journey by the enemy or 2) the stronghold God's word has on the heart of the righteous. Both are significant as we prepare to conclude this 21-day fast. We Rebuke, Resist, and Reject the strongholds of the enemy. Fasting breaks the cycle and chains of strongholds. "This is done only by prayer and fasting" (Matthew 17:21). Fasting also enhances our relationship with God. We willingly bind our hearts to His word and find delight in His ways (verse 143). Today we multitask: we Resist strongholds and Rest in our salvation. Here we Go!

"Sunrise, Time" QOPH (Hebrew)

145 I cried with my whole heart; hear me, O LORD: I will keep thy statutes. 146 I cried unto thee; save me, and I shall keep thy testimonies. 147 I prevented the dawning of the morning, and cried: I hoped in thy word. 148 Mine eyes prevent the night watches, that I might meditate in thy word. 149 Hear my voice according unto thy lovingkindness: O LORD, quicken me according to thy judgment. 150 They draw nigh that follow after mischief: they are far from thy law. 151 Thou art near, O LORD; and all thy commandments are truth. 152 Concerning thy testimonies, I have known of old that thou hast founded them for ever.

Psalm 119:145-152

Rise and Shine! The letter Q in Hebrew is a picture of the Sun rising in the horizon. The circle represents the sun and the tail of the "q" represents the movement of the sun rising. Today it's time for us to rise! We rise above our previous low expectations. We expect results from this fast! We expect movement in the heavens and manifestation on earth. Your time with God has not been wasted (verses 147, 148). Let's rise today. Get up! Get going! Shake things up! We make fasting attractive, and our anointing is contagious! Rise! Here we Go!

"Head, Chief"
RESH (Hebrew)

¹⁵³ Consider mine affliction, and deliver me: for I do not forget thy law. ¹⁵⁴ Plead my cause, and deliver me: quicken me according to thy word. ¹⁵⁵ Salvation is far from the wicked: for they seek not thy statutes. ¹⁵⁶ Great are thy tender mercies, O LORD: quicken me according to thy judgments. ¹⁵⁷ Many are my persecutors and mine enemies; yet do I not decline from thy testimonies. ¹⁵⁸ I beheld the transgressors, and was grieved; because they kept not thy word. ¹⁵⁹ Consider how I love thy precepts: quicken me, O LORD, according to thy lovingkindness. ¹⁶⁰ Thy word is true from the beginning: and every one of thy righteous judgments endureth for ever.

Psalm 119:153-160

Today, we pray for those who have authority. We pray for the heads of households, supervisors, teachers, principals, pastors, the judicial system, law enforcement, and the president. During biblical times, many kings and rulers misused their authority. The psalmist pleads for God's word to rule (verse 158). As this is still relevant today, we can't forget that our prayers have power: "If my people, who are called by my name, will humble themselves and pray and seek my face and turn from their wicked ways, then I will hear from heaven, and I will forgive their sin and will heal their land" (2 Chronicles. 7:14). We are called to pray for leaders (1 Tim. 2:1-3). Remember your prayer has power. Here we Go!

Week 5: Midnight Message
A NET-BREAKING EXPERIENCE

Hey, we're here again with your message at midnight. I hope you've had an amazing day. As we always say, this is our time to sit back, to hear a quick word, and to prepare ourselves to get a good night's sleep. I'm so glad that you're taking this journey with me. You will not believe how outside of myself this whole process has been

Tonight we're going to come from Luke chapter 5. But before we get there, there's something I want you to think about and consider. I want you to consider when was the last time you had a net-breaking experience? When was the last time that you were so abundantly full and you were so abundantly blessed that you had to share with somebody? When was the last time that you had to give out of your abundance and not out of your lack? Tonight, we're going to talk a little bit about a net-breaking experience.

When we start thinking about a net-breaking experience, we are going to look at how Jesus had an encounter with Simon when He told him to launch out into the deep. But before we get there, I have a quick testimony to share. In one of our other midnight messages, I told you about some friends of mine and the cruise we went on. Remember, I didn't want to go on the cruise. But here I was, out on this big ship. Not only did they convince me to go on this cruise, but now they said we had to take an excursion. I didn't even know what that was because this was my first cruise. But I said okay.

We started talking about the things we could do, and we waited until the very last minute. Suddenly we decided to go on an excursion. So, we get off the ship only to get on another boat. I looked at my good friends and let them know I didn't want to get on one boat, and now they have me on another. So, I'm on the tour boat and the tour guide was directing and taking us to the excursion. It was an excursion inside of an excursion. So, we are in the middle of this big lake and the tour guide tells us that this is our stop. I'm looking around and saying to myself, *where's our stop? I don't see any land; I don't see anything.* He said the boat is on the other side.

I began to look at my friends and said to myself *I got to get new friends. I am not messing with you all.* So, we get off from this boat only to board what they call a mini submarine so that we can go under water and see the fish and the coral. The boat had to go out far into the deep. So, as I was complaining and fearful, by the time I got down to the mini submarine and got to the bottom of that boat so I could see the bottom of the ocean, it was so beautiful. But I could only see what I saw if I was willing to launch out into the deep. I could only see what I saw if I was willing to get on to 3 different boats so I could see the bottom of this beautiful ocean, that looked like another world underneath. I was so glad that I did it. But I couldn't have experienced it unless I launched out into the deep.

So, what's our revelation for tonight? Let's go to Luke 5:4. It speaks about Jesus and His encounter with Simon. It says, "Now when he had left speaking, he said unto Simon, Launch out into the deep, and let down your nets for a draught." It sounds really simple, but He said this to Simon at a time when Simon was tired. He said this to Simon at a time when Simon had already been perplexed. He said it at a time when Simon had already let Him borrow his boat so that Jesus could do His sermon—so that He could preach. This sounds a little like my friends —come get on this boat, come on get on this boat until I was out in the deep.

I want to tell you right now that even though you may be feeling perplexed, and you may be feeling a little bit tired, be like Simon and follow Jesus' instructions just because it is Jesus who said it. We've been fishing all night long and we are already tired, and we are just washing our nets. Now you're asking us to go back to a place where we've already been disappointed, to go back to a place where we've already experienced fear, and where we've already experienced lack? But we are going to do it just because You say so.

Listen, even if you have to do it with an attitude, even if you have to do it with a little bit of fear like myself, just do it anyway. Because when Simon went out in the middle of that ocean, when he went out into the deep, he caught so many fish that his net began to break. I want to tell you we are one moment away from a net-breaking experience. We are one moment away from God doing something so extraordinary in our life that we are going to have to call our friends, we'll have to call people to come and help us because if they don't help us our boat is going to sink. You are about to be so blessed that you are about to have a net-breaking experience. I know you've washed your nets, I know that you're already tired, I know that you've already pulled your boat on shore, but guess what, you were created for this. You are a fisherman, go out and catch something and don't catch what you already got, go do something different; go out into the deep because Jesus says so.

And maybe that's the difference. Maybe we've been in shallow waters for too long. Maybe we haven't cast our nets out in this kind of water. When Jesus said go out into the deep, you'll experience something you've never experienced before. I want to encourage you tonight, before you go to bed, to get ready for a net-breaking experience.

"Eat, Teeth"
SHIN (Hebrew)

¹⁶¹ *Princes have persecuted me without a cause: but my heart standeth in awe of thy word.* ¹⁶² *I rejoice at thy word, as one that findeth great spoil.* ¹⁶³ *I hate and abhor lying: but thy law do I love.* ¹⁶⁴ *Seven times a day do I praise thee because of thy righteous judgments.*
¹⁶⁵ *Great peace have they which love thy law: and nothing shall offend them.* ¹⁶⁶ *LORD, I have hoped for thy salvation, and done thy commandments.* ¹⁶⁷ *My soul hath kept thy testimonies; and I love them exceedingly.* ¹⁶⁸ *I have kept thy precepts and thy testimonies: for all my ways are before thee.*

Psalm 119:161-168

God has an amazing sense of humor. The 21st letter presented in the Hebrew is "eat" or "teeth." Don't get too excited . . . it's not just about food. It's to be sharp, press in, and to have precision. Today, don't rush to go back to physical food, but think about what you will feast on in the spirit. What will come out of your mouth and through your teeth? The psalmist declared, "Seven times a day do I praise thee" (verse 164). Some of us eat that many times a day. Will we intentionally praise Him that many times? Today, as we close out our fast, Remember to Feast on His Word, Love, and Compassion. Thank you for taking the journey! Keep Pressing! Here we Go!

Happy Day 21 everyone. I am so excited for you who decided to take the 21-day fast with Angel White Ministries.

So, this morning, before you get started, I just wanted to encourage you. I just want to let you know that your fast doesn't have to end today. The level of anointing that you need, the level of deliverance that you need in your life, and the level of power that you want to operate in, is the level of consecration, prayer, and fasting that you have to continue throughout the entire year. In Matthew 17:21 it says, "This kind only comes by prayer and fasting."

So today, make the decision to make prayer and fasting your lifestyle. You can do it one day each week, one week each month, or day each month. But whatever you do, stay consecrated.

Next Step: Final Midnight Message
God Will Give You More

Good evening, here we are. It's midnight and I am excited to share a quick word with you.

Tonight, I just want to encourage someone who feels like they are on the brink of something great but you just need one more good push or a few more good pushes. I started to think about my grandmother today and her tenacity, her greatness. I know a lot of people think their grandmothers are great, but my grandmother is amazing. She is a demonstration of not only beauty but of God's Grace. And I watch her. I watch how she handles the word of God in her preaching. I watch how she handles herself as an older single woman so beautiful and yet so plain and simple and so powerful.

There's one thing my grandmother does that she has done for years, and I didn't quite understand it until I had to go through my own process. Every single week without fail—she may change the day according to what her plans are for the week—but one day out of every single week for as long as I can remember my grandmother has fasted. She calls it her shut-in day. This is the day where she cuts herself off from everybody. She doesn't come out of her room and she doesn't eat anything until later on in the evening. She spends that day in the word of God. How many of us can do that? Some of us can't even afford to do that as we are not retired and have so many obligations. But for my grandmother, even if we're travelling and on vacation together, she takes one day out of each week to seek God's face.

So, one of the things I started doing for myself is I have moments when I am on a continual fast, like an extended fast. It may be giving up sweets, it may be giving up meat, it may be not eating after a certain time, but I'm always trying to set aside a moment of self-sacrifice, if you will. Why do I allow God to have His space and His time in my life? Because grandmother taught me that's her moment to hear from God.

What is our revelation for tonight's message at midnight? Let's look at Daniel 1:15. It says, "And at the end of ten days their countenances appeared fairer and fatter in flesh than all the children which did eat the portion of the king's meat." Verse 17 says, "As for these four children, God gave them knowledge and skill in all learning and wisdom: and Daniel had understanding in all visions and dreams." Did you get that?

Listen, tonight, I want to talk about how God will give you more. Sometimes, when we talk about God giving us more, we start thinking about houses, cars, and things that are manifested in the natural. But here, we understand that Daniel and these men—Hananiah, Mishael and Azariah; you know them as Meshack, Shadrack and Abednego—decided that they were not going to eat from the King's table. They decided that when they ate, they were going to eat vegetables, drink plenty of water, and that they weren't going to eat choice meat to drink wine. They had decided what their diet was going to be because they knew they had to hear from God; they knew they had to be in a position to give wisdom and understanding, and so they fasted. They decided to set aside something so that they could hear from God. Are you wanting to hear from God? Are you at a place in your life where you need a little more direction? It's midnight, it's late You've already worked all day long, but there may be something lingering and you're saying, "God, I need to hear from You. God, I need a revelation, God I need Your direction." If this is the case, if you really need something extra from God, if you really need this extra push then just maybe, you ought to consider fasting.

Pick a fast, any fast. You can fast from TV, you can fast from food, you can fast from certain beverages. You can fast for a certain amount of hours or days. I just believe that if grandmamma says it works, and Daniel says it works, then it works. Set aside that time and I believe that God will give you more. Not necessarily more of what's manifested in the natural, but He may give you more wisdom, skill, and understanding; that's what we need. That's what we all desire.

So, as we get ready for bedtime tonight, just understand that maybe God is pushing you, maybe God is pushing us, to give up something so that He can give us more. I want to encourage you that maybe another fast is in your future.

God bless you. I'll see you on the other side of midnight.

ABOUT THE AUTHOR

Dr. Angel E. White graduated from Virginia State University where she received a Bachelors of Science degree in Business Marketing. She is also a graduate of Virginia Union University, Samuel Dewitt Proctor School of Theology with a Masters of Divinity degree. She holds an earned Doctoral degree in Management & Organizational Leadership from the University of Phoenix, School of Advanced Studies.

Dr. White is the Founder of Faithful Rebuilders. This ministry hosts family conferences and retreats. She is also a 3-time self-published author of book titles including: A Woman of Worth, In The Beginning God, and The Seed in My Pocket (A Children's Book).

Dr. Angel White serves as the Youth Pastor at Good Shepherd Baptist Church located in Petersburg, Virginia, where Bishop Jeffrey L. Reaves Sr. serves as the Senior Pastor.

OTHER BOOKS BY THE AUTHOR

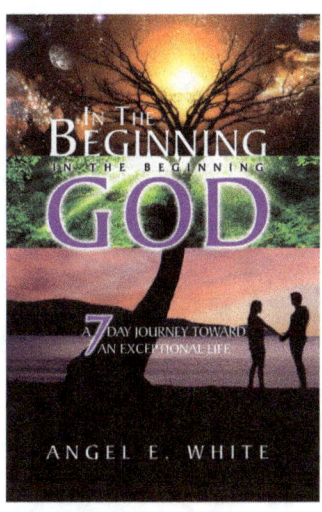

Available at www.angelwhite.org

www.ingramcontent.com/pod-product-compliance
Lightning Source LLC
Chambersburg PA
CBHW052120070526
44584CB00017B/2573